Poems
and
Prayers
for the
Seasons

Published by Trinity Books
An Imprint of Trinity North Shore
on Boston's North Shore
www.trinitynorthsore.org/trinitybooks

Softcover Print ISBN: 979-8-218-56008-9
Hardcover Print ISBN: 979-8-218-56009-6
Digital ISBN: 979-8-218-69530-9

Print LCCN 2025911272

Interior Design by Nelly Murariu at PixBeeDesign.com
Cover Design by Pete Whitten
Watercolor Images by Beth Coombes

Printed in the United States of America

Poems and Prayers for the Seasons

A Guided Journal to Help You Pay Attention
to the World Around You, the Life Within You,
and Embrace the Gifts of Every Season

JENNIFER A. DRUMMOND

Contents

Foreword   x

Introduction   xv

WINTER   **1**

Introductory Poem: No One Told Me   8

Week 1: Waiting   11

  Week 1 Poem: Advent Haiku   12

  Week 1, Day 1   13

  Week 1, Day 2   14

  Week 1, Day 3   15

  Week 1, Day 4   16

  Week 1, Day 5   17

Week 2: Watching (with Hope)   19

  Week 2 Poem: Snowy Morning   20

  Week 2, Day 1   21

  Week 2, Day 2   22

  Week 2, Day 3   23

  Week 2, Day 4   24

  Week 2, Day 5   25

Week 3: Celebrating   27

  Week 3 Poem: Holidays   28

  Week 3, Day 1   29

  Week 3, Day 2   30

  Week 3, Day 3   31

  Week 3, Day 4   32

  Week 3, Day 5   33

Week 4: Waiting (in Darkness)   35
   Week 4 Poem: In the afternoon   36
   Week 4, Day 1   37
   Week 4, Day 2   38
   Week 4, Day 3   39
   Week 4, Day 4   40
   Week 4, Day 5   41

Bonus Sunshine Prayers   42

SPRING   **47**
Introductory Poem: On a lilac   51

Week 1: Beginnings   53
   Week 1 Poem: Beckoning   54
   Week 1, Day 1   55
   Week 1, Day 2   56
   Week 1, Day 3   57
   Week 1, Day 4   58
   Week 1, Day 5   59

Week 2: Toiling   61
   Week 2 Poem: Ashes   62
   Week 2, Day 1   63
   Week 2, Day 2   64
   Week 2, Day 3   65
   Week 2, Day 4   66
   Week 2, Day 5   67

Week 3: Waiting   69
   Week 3 Poem: March is Mid   70
   Week 3, Day 1   72
   Week 3, Day 2   73
   Week 3, Day 3   74
   Week 3, Day 4   75
   Week 3, Day 5   76

Week Four: Rising   77
    Week 4 Poem: The Flowering of the Cross (or what
    comes after)   78
    Week 4, Day 1   80
    Week 4, Day 2   81
    Week 4, Day 3   82
    Week 4, Day 4   83
    Week 4, Day 5   84

Bonus Transition to Summer Poem: There Comes
a Moment   85

SUMMER   **87**
Introductory Poem: Sitting with Grandma   91

Week 1: Beauty   93
    Week 1 Poem: On a Strawberry   94
    Week 1, Day 1   95
    Week 1, Day 2   96
    Week 1, Day 3   97
    Week 1, Day 4   98
    Week 1, Day 5   99

Week 2: Play   101
    Week 2 Poem: Bike ride   102
    Week 2, Day 1   104
    Week 2, Day 2   105
    Week 2, Day 3   106
    Week 2, Day 4   107
    Week 2, Day 5   108

Week 3: Rest   109
    Week 3 Poem: Penny, who is lying in the sun   110
    Week 3, Day 1   111
    Week 3, Day 2   112

Week 3, Day 3   113
Week 3, Day 4   114
Week 3, Day 5   115

Week 4: Connection   117
Week 4 Poem: the way the ocean pulls   118
Week 4, Day 1   119
Week 4, Day 2   120
Week 4, Day 3   121
Week 4, Day 4   122
Week 4, Day 5   123

Bonus Benedictions   124

AUTUMN   **127**
Introductory Poem: Crystal Moments (On being 13) 132

Week 1: Equilibrium   135
Week 1 Poem: Caim (circle of protection)   136
Week 1, Day 1   138
Week 1, Day 2   139
Week 1, Day 3   140
Week 1, Day 4   141
Week 1, Day 5   142

Week 2: Change   143
Week 2 Poem: the way the leaves light and dance   144
Week 2, Day 1   145
Week 2, Day 2   146
Week 2, Day 3   147
Week 2, Day 4   148
Week 2, Day 5   149

Week 3: Gather   151
Week 3 Poem: On a Pomegranate   152
Week 3, Day 1   153

Week 3, Day 2   154
Week 3, Day 3   155
Week 3, Day 4   156
Week 3, Day 5   157

Week 4: Release   159
Week 4 Poem: Bedtime on a Sunday   160
Week 4, Day 1   162
Week 4, Day 2   163
Week 4, Day 3   164
Week 4, Day 4   165
Week 4, Day 5   166

Endings and Beginnings   167
Acknowledgments   175
Resources to Help You Further Embrace the Seasons   179
About the Author   180
About the Artist   181

Foreword

Jennifer Drummond has a gift for poetry—for its rhythms, its quiet and quiet-ing. For its joy or nostalgia, its ability to get behind our defenses before delivering a surprise. More than that, she has that rare, wonderful gift that perhaps makes poetry possible: she is able to sit in solitude and silence in the beauty— small or large—of all that is, to see and delight and be filled with wonder. She is able both to live life and to observe and to ponder it all at once.

This volume offers something that is not easy to find in our distracted and much-disheveled times: it offers a thread we can weave into our lives for a year; a beautiful and delightful core thread that, as in a classic tweed, may at times show its color forth and be upfront—a poem or an insight we just have to share with friends. At other times, this thread may be hidden amongst the many pressing responsibilities and opportunities, yet still be present, even just to our own inner selves, our centered time with God. Finally, that continuing thread through the whole of a year may allow us to develop something of the gift that Jennifer has herself: an inner space that is not hurried and scurried and thinned but is warm and alive and vibrant. Walking through the seasons with Jennifer, as she has so kindly offered to guide us on pilgrimage, may allow us to mark and note the days and weeks and turns as we live through them, savoring life and having emotional-spiritual resources for what it brings, of whatever sort.

I believe that this sort of consistent reflecting and growing of wonder is not something else added to the list, but a resource giving the means to be able to face the list, day in and day out. It is the possibility of coming to the end of a year and not wondering where it went, but of looking back upon a path that is familiar.

One note of caution (although perhaps that is too strong a word): the hurried life offers us seeming protection from the slings and arrows of outrageous fortune and unexpected hardships. On the contrast, solitude, prayer, and wonder tend rather to open us up, tend to remove that protection, in a good way. It is possible that walking the year through this volume will invoke deep emotions, perhaps of joy, grief, or, of course, something else. It is not a risk-free path, but it is a path to depth of life.

When people come to me for pastoral care in a time of grief, they sometimes wonder if what they are feeling is reasonable or too much. They wonder if they are losing hold. I tell them that they are, in fact, very much sane. I assure them that this assurance alone is perhaps the deepest note of respect I could give to them in a time when many would turn to denial or some other way that would be other than real.

It may be that what you find here is strong medicine. But the strong medicine here is not grief. No, it is wonder and delight.

Tim Clayton

Beverly Farms
Eastertide 2024

The Ordinary Tree

Six twenty-five a.m. and we sit in the chapel,
Bleary-eyed, psalm after psalm, sleepy child on my lap
and outside the open window is a tree.

The leaves do not warrant a passing glance—
plain old green with a few crab apples,
not good for flinging, limbs not worthy of a summertime climb.
Even Kujo, the terrier too small for his name, rarely marks his
territory here.
Yet with the cool morning breeze, the quiet stillness,
it's as if God himself whispers, "Look at me," and the
leaves rustle.
The green leaves brim with life, the crab apples invite a
thrower, and the limbs beckon a climber.
For a moment the ordinary has become extraordinary.

Another morning in the chapel, windows only cracked
against the chill.
The leaves hang on, mud brown and sour yellow. The harsh
wind foretells cold,
and its rough voice rasps gloom.
Yet later, when the sun dips at the horizon, the world is
bathed in gold.

The tree is lit from God's own glory and cries, "Look at me!"
Mud brown becomes a wondrous earthy shade and tangy
yellow becomes a sweet promise.
For a moment the ordinary has become extraordinary.

The chapel windows are double-sealed, and no one is
without slippers.
The tree whips in the dark wind; in the pre-dawn we cannot
see the branches.
Yet midday when the snow has fallen and the branches bear
the burden lightly,
my kids notice the pure, white load on the limbs, a fairyland.
God reminds, "Look at me." His burden is light, and
for a moment the ordinary has become extraordinary.

The dawn creeps forward as do the psalms,
there are grey sticks where there should be buds,
no visible green.
Yet our morning walk and close inspection reveal
teeny-tiny almost green spots. God tenderly calls, "Look at me,"
trust for life when there seems none.
The ordinary has become extraordinary.

Introduction

Mill Street House

About fifteen years ago we lived in a classic New England triple decker, three apartments stacked on top of one another. We and our children, ages three and one, were invited to live in this house, an "intentional liturgical community." A priest friend and her husband occupied the first floor while various combinations of single folks, married couples, and families rented the other two floors. We practiced living together in community; we agreed to pray a service called *Morning Prayer* (from the *Book of Common Prayer*) Monday through Friday mornings, and another service called *Compline* at 9 p.m. each night. We also agreed to eat a meal together once a week. Other than that, we would go about our daily lives working, parenting, attending classes, whatever it was that we were doing at that stage of life.

There were times when this was really great—fun conversations or impromptu game nights, for example. There were times when this turned out to be helpful—built-in babysitting options, getting a ride to the airport, or borrowing a cup of sugar and then sharing the cookies. There were times when this was quite boring—when we prayed the psalms at 6:25 a.m. for what felt like the 1000th time, or when we had a house meeting about tying our trash bags before throwing them in the dumpster. There were also times when this was downright painful—for example, when we painted a mural on a wall that it turns out wasn't ours to paint.

The Seasons Are About Movement

Life ebbs and flows, moving from one season to another. During that season at Mill Street House, this was most exemplified for me by a tree that stood outside the chapel window. I would watch this tree, morning after morning, and notice the subtle changes.

As the weather morphed, I noticed the tree outside with its buds, barely visible in early spring, growing into leaves that reminded me of the power of God to bring life. I also noticed what was happening in the chapel where we prayed. As the weather warmed up and the tree leafed out, we shed slippers and long sleeves, toes free to wiggle and arms bare to feel sunlight through the window. With the shift to fall and the golden orange of the leaves outside, I noticed sweatshirts and coffee mugs appearing, signs of coziness. In the middle of winter, I knew the tree was there but couldn't see it in pre-dawn; but I could see the quilts upon laps in the dim room.

We passed two years in that house with several rounds of friends coming and going. We left, a moving van full of stuff, hearts full of memories, and heads full of experiences to ponder. That was the beginning for me of paying attention to the seasons around me. We made several moves, and in each new space I would watch for the light—where did it enter in the day and leave in the evening? How did the view from my window change over time? What ways did I tend to mark the passing of seasons, of time? How could I be more intentional about this as more and more time passed, and our children were growing up at what felt like warp speed?

Seasons happen whether we want them to or not. We have no control over them, only how we respond to them. We can ignore them, we can resent them and resist them, or we can embrace them. If we choose to embrace them and pay attention to them, they have gifts to offer us. The seasons tell us about life, about ourselves, and about God.

The flow of the seasons, like the tide, reminds us that change happens. We don't need to fear it, or even worse, resist it by trying to move backwards to a previous season. In fact, we do more damage in the search for what was then if we move in sync with the changes. We don't have to love or even like the changes, but to have an awareness of seasonal change is to acknowledge reality. It is to be on a growth trajectory.

Seasons Teach Us About the External and Internal Life

Beyond the flow from one to the next, each season reminds us of things that are true. Spring reminds us with all its extravagance, the colors, the sounds, the fragrance, that life begins anew. There is hope! The extravagance of spring shows us God's extravagant love for not just the world but for each of us individually.

Summer speaks to us of beauty and rest, work and play. We see evidence of growth and the greening power of God.[1] Summer reveals God's pleasure and delight in growing things, and his power to transform barren places into lush gardens.

Autumn brings the fruition of our hope and our work, the harvest, and alerts us to great change coming, as leaves fall and light wanes. When we feel parts of ourselves or our lives are stripped away, we are reminded of the falling leaves—if the tree did not release these, it would not survive the winter.

---

1   The German Abbess Saint Hildegard coined the phrase *veriditas* in the Middle Ages, this sense of the spirit of God making things green from the inside out - breathing life into us the same way each spring the world leafs out in green.

Winter teaches us about sabbath, about waiting and trusting, and how little we can do to speed or change the process. When the landscape is white and barren, we are reminded that those creatures who hibernate are protected in the cold and the darkness. This leads to spring, and the cycle begins again.

Seasons Repeat, Reinforce, and Remind Us

In the winter of 2020, before Covid shut down the world, I ran my first retreat about wintertime. Fourteen brave souls gathered in the coffee shop for a chilly morning together, and I shared the "Ordinary Tree" poem. This started a lively and ongoing conversation with many of the retreat attendees—which led to a retreat for every season, and a group that met between retreats to continue the discussion about how to keep noticing God and the seasons on an ongoing basis.

This also began a period for me of intensely noticing both my external and internal landscapes. As I spent time observing the world around me in preparation for these retreats, I began to notice my own internal rhythms—times when I would feel renewed hope or see signs of growth and life. Other times felt harder as I was asked to relinquish habits or ideas that no longer served me. And sometimes all felt bleak and quiet.

This book is a product of at least the last fifteen years. But once I began paying attention, I couldn't help but think back through my life and particular scents and sights of different seasons: dainty petit fours and pastel Easter eggs on Grandma Jeanne's dining room table in childhood; teenage summer evenings full of fresh-cut grass and petunias, the sun slowly sinking; carving pumpkins with college friends; crunching snow underfoot as my husband and I explored small towns in Vermont for the first time.

These particular memories, contours of my life experience, help me to know what life and what God are like. You have your own lifetime of gathered seasons to sift through and remember. Here is my prayer and hope for you, dear reader, as you enter into this practice:

> *May you be encouraged to continue your journey, paying attention to the seasons—to the beauty, to God—all around you now. May you be blessed as you look back to find joy and God in unexpected places along the way. And may you find these things even more deeply as you move forward in your life, paying closer attention.*

A Note About How to Use This Book

These words, prayers, and poems are offered to help you to turn to God and see all the beauty in this huge and wonderful world. You may choose to skim through it, lingering with any page that catches your eye or your heart. You may open it at the beginning of the season, find that it is not sitting well, and shelve it for a later time. You may find particular passages that speak to you all year or "out of season." In any of these instances, I am delighted that these words find you there and pray God does too.

If you are like me and find predictable rhythms helpful in your life, I have crafted this especially for you! You'll notice that there is a general introduction—you may have already read it. If not, I suggest you do so that you can begin to consider how the seasons speak to us both about our internal and external life. This can be read anytime, should be read repeatedly, and is suitable for beginning each season.

There are four seasons that correspond to the four natural seasons: winter, spring, summer, and fall. Each season has an introduction to it and has a guiding question that can be pondered the whole season long. There is also an introductory poem for each season that you can come back to throughout the season to help remind you of both the arc and the peculiarities of each season.

Each season is broken into four weeks. Each week has a set of questions for you to consider that help unpack the guiding question for the season, and then each week has five collects (prayers that help "collect" us around one particular theme). For this book I have used something from nature to remind us of something about God and ourselves and to make one request.[2]

You will notice I include the dictionary definition of the theme for the week.[3] For example, in Week 1, Day 1 of winter, the theme is waiting. The definition of waiting is *the action of staying where one is or delaying action until a particular time or until something else happens.* I find this helpful, because then I can consider what action am I delaying and what am I waiting for? I ask myself this question over the course of the season, and I notice how my answer may shift from the beginning of winter to the end of it.

---

2 Padrig O'Tuma's delightful book *Praying with Corymela*, especially his introduction, is instrumental in my understanding of these kinds of prayers and the impetus for my own practice of writing them.

3 I provide the dictionary meaning from dictionary.com

There is ample space in this book for you to doodle, draw, or otherwise engage in a creative response to the season. You may want to write your own collects or prayers, you may wish to write your own thoughts and responses to what you see around you, or you may leave it blank to appreciate the white space, intended to give your mind and soul a little breathing room.

A Note About the Illustrations

The images in this book are intended to support your work of noticing the seasons. Each one is an invitation to practice looking softly, to pause, to let yourself get lost in beauty. Don't rush, but savor as you are able, devoting time and attention, considering the colors, the lines, the marvel that each one is. Use them as inspiration to pursue your own creative response, sit with them quietly in prayer, learn to appreciate the hard work of the artist, share your favorite with a friend, or even better, take the chance to sit outside and observe the world around you!

Winter

The Church[4] has a liturgical calendar which orients us to the birth, life and ministry, death, and resurrection of Jesus. The Church year begins with Advent, the four weeks before Christmas, when we slow down and prepare ourselves, our hearts, and our homes for the arrival of Jesus. The Twelve Days of Christmas, twelve days of feasting and celebrating Jesus' arrival on earth, begin December 25th and last until January 6th, when we celebrate the arrival of the Three Wise Men. This is the season of Epiphany.[5] The word Epiphany itself means "appearance," and the season signifies that God's light has come for everyone. Jesus, the Light of the world, goes out so that everyone may see and come to God. This season of Epiphany lasts until late winter/early spring and ends on Ash Wednesday.[6]

It makes sense, if you follow the Church year, to begin at the beginning, waiting for a birth. But what about the natural seasons? Why start with winter, a perhaps plain season and the darkest time of the year?

I heard at some point how Jewish families would have their celebrations with a dinner at sundown, but I always thought that notion really wasn't relevant to my Christian faith. But at a conference once, I heard a speaker talk about how when God created the world, he separated darkness

---

4   I use "the Church" here to mean those of the Christian faith—Catholics, Protestants and Orthodox—who may have slight variations in how they follow this calendar but who all have some sort of pattern to help their people both understand and live into the realities of Jesus' life, his teachings, his death and resurrection, and the arrival of the Holy Spirit.

5   There are a few celebratory days in this time period where the Church marks moments of Jesus' childhood—his presentation in the Temple, his Baptism.

6   Ash Wednesday begins the penitential season of Lent, the forty days before Easter. The dates of Easter, and thus Lent, vary year to year, based on the date of the first Sunday after the first full moon after the vernal equinox. Lucky for us our calendars have it marked!

and light; *there was evening and there was morning, the first day* and so on through all the days. What a realization that this didn't only apply to my Jewish friends and family but applied to my life of faith as well!

The person went on to say this was a revolutionary way to think about patterns of life because it means that we start in darkness. He meant it literally—we began life in our mother's womb, in total darkness. He also meant that if each day begins at sundown, we have a whole night to surrender to unconsciousness and trust that God will wake us in the morning, with the dawn. We practice a little death each night and practice a little resurrection each morning—all in preparation for our own end, death and resurrection.

If all this is true, when I wake up in the morning, God has been actively at work all night long, in the darkness. All I have to do is rise and join him. I can't tell you how waking with this understanding and perspective has radically changed how I see my to-do list! Many (though not all) days I am able to begin with a sense of anticipation rather than crushing guilt at being behind before I even get out of bed.

Thus, we are starting with winter on purpose. Though you can start with any season—and I do think you should jump in whatever season you are in (for heaven's sake, don't wait until winter to start just because I picked it as a starting place!) —there is something both symbolic and real that happens when we start in the darkest part of the year, acknowledging our helplessness and dependence on God.

A Season of "Barrenness" and Waiting

Winter can seem a time of "less": less sunshine, less fresh food, lower temperatures, fewer leaves on the trees. The landscape is bleaker, clearer. It can seem a time of barrenness, when nothing is able to grow. Frozen ground and weak light prohibit it (at least in the North). It is often associated with barrenness—nothing is visible or happening on the surface.

One winter I was pregnant, my daughter was born in March. That experience began to change how I viewed this "barren" time—while nothing was happening on the surface, I was very aware of the changes that were happening within my body. Then I read this:

> All around us we observe a pregnant creation. The difficult times of pain throughout the world are simply birth pangs. But it's not only around us; it's within us. The Spirit of God is arousing us within. We're also feeling the birth pangs. These sterile and barren bodies of ours are yearning for full deliverance. **That is why waiting does not diminish us, any more than waiting diminishes a pregnant mother. We are enlarged in the waiting.** We, of course, don't see what is enlarging us. But the longer we wait, the larger we become, and the more joyful our expectancy.
>
> (Romans 8:22-25 MSG, emphasis mine)

This was a profound realization: being pregnant is a really good analogy for how to wait!

A Season of Darkness and Protection

Just as a human needs nine months of darkness and protection to grow, so do other things. Consider the bulbs planted in the fall that remain under the frozen earth all winter long. They need the time of darkness to prepare for the warmer temperature and light of spring which will cause them to sprout. Ponder the animals that hibernate— the bear, the hedgehog, the tiny mouse or the water-loving frog. All these are protected by the darkness; what may initially seem a burden turns out to actually be a gift. As a part of the cycle of the seasons, the darkness provides safety and security that a creature needs to prepare for the "resurrection" of the coming season.

Thinking about waiting as preserving a dark and nourishing space for something to be born has changed how I experience winter. Now, when I am morose or melancholy with another cold day or another early sunset, I imagine something small and precious growing bigger. I imagine myself enlarged in this waiting, my heart and my capacity for love expanding.

A Final Note

I live in the northeastern United States (and grew up in the Midwest). Thus, my experiences of winter have been shaped by darkness and bleak landscapes. It's an exquisitely beautiful time of year and there are gifts aplenty, but not everyone has the same light and weather changes as I do. My mother, for example, lives in Florida, and our experiences seem to be opposite—when it's too cold to be outside up here, she is there enjoying the pleasant breezes. And when she is sweltering, unable to bear the heat outside, we are enjoying pleasant temperatures.

I'm also keenly aware as I write this in the fall of 2023 that many regions of the country are suffering from what had been the hottest summer on record, along with rare flooding, wildfires, and draughts that are unfortunately becoming more common as the climate changes. This awareness has inspired me to pray fervently for our earth, and for my own participation in its degradation or restoration. May your observations and experiences of the natural world lead you to deeper prayer, especially if you are experiencing changing weather and traumatic weather events.

The prayers and poems of this book are born out of my own experiences, the landscapes that I did and do inhabit, and I pray they may be an invitation for you to consider and observe your own landscapes. What is and has winter been like for you, and how can those experiences shape your own prayers?

Question to Consider in Winter: What Are You Waiting For?

As you are aware of particular sights, sounds, and smells this winter, I invite you to go deeper and ask what these gifts might want to say to you. Let this question for the season guide you, provide a touchpoint for you to keep coming back to as you experience this season and reflect on all that unfolds.

INTRODUCTORY POEM

No One Told Me

No one told me that until she was born, time would stop.

Those pregnant moments of my pregnant life ticked by.

How could the Red Sox play ball? (And win?!) How could the weatherman point to clouds and sun—again? How could she talk about dinner, and he talk about indigestion, when inside of me, life quickened, and fluttered...and began? Hurry up! I screamed silently, as my very fingers itched, and my toes wiggled in restless anticipation and my heart murmured with every beat: *Who are you? When will you be here? Why must I wait?* The clock tocked on and on and on.

The beeps and thrums of machines in the room provided a steady soundtrack for life's emergence. Discomfort. Beep. Breathe. Beep. Pain. Beep. Squeeze. Beep. Push. She's HERE! Beep beep. But time didn't stop—it fast-forwarded, because in a flurry of blankets and balloons, we were home.

Everyone told me when she was little that time would fly.

Those blurry moments of a blurry life ticked by.

She needs
food and
I need
food. She's
sleeping and
I should do the
dishes. She's crying and
I'm crying. She's dressed
and I need a shower. I close
my eyes for a nap and how much
can one baby poop?
The moments crawl forward at a mind-numbing pace
and I cry, Hurry up! My fingers are anxious to do
something, anything besides nurturing growth, and my
toes curl, uncurl as I settle in, to nurse for 45 minutes
that takes ten years. Time doesn't fly—it winds and
slithers and inches forward, barely.

And then, wrapping paper and cupcake-paper crinkle
in celebration. Two whole years, measured now not in
weeks or months. We can hardly imagine how we got
here. Time hasn't flown; it careened around the years,
leaving us breathless with its speed.

Suddenly someone tells me—and I hear it. My heart
swells at the thought of it and yes. I can try to live into
this, without crying "Hurry!" or grasping sadly, wondering
how to keep the moment; the days are long, but the
years are short.

WAITING

Verb: the action of staying where one is or delaying action until a particular time or until something else happens.

Questions to Consider This Week

As you ponder *what you are waiting for*, I invite you to read the following poem. Are you able to easily identify what you are waiting for? Can you articulate some part of this waiting? What might you need to scale back from in order to see more clearly?

Week 1 Poem: Advent Haiku

In a season of fullness,
to scale back requires work and faith;
freedom to fully see.

Week 1, Day 1

God of the river rocks,
Those polished stones
Smoothed by the pressure
of water and time,
Colorful circles that cry out your praise
When we are silent;
Grant us patience as time and the waters of love
Flow over us, that
Our colorful selves may be revealed.
For your creation praises you
By being its fully formed self.
Amen.

Week 1, Day 2

God of the rising sun
That daily reminder of your faithfulness
That sometimes blazes a fiery announcement
Sometimes peeps over as a shy lover
And sometimes is obscured as a bride behind her veil;
Grant us eyes to see your arrival
In whatever form you come,
And help our hearts to receive you
In fire, in shyness, and in hiding.
For you appeared to your people in all these ways
And we are changed by your appearing.
Amen.

Week 1, Day 3

O God of the waiting,
You who waited nine months to be born
Who waited years to begin your public works
Who waited generations to come for your purposes of love;
Give us the gift of trust
As we enter our own waiting,
Months for an answer
Years for growth and preparation
And at our end, let us fling ourselves upon you
As have generations before us.
For your purposes are always of love and
We are always the recipients.
Amen.

Week 1, Day 4

O God of the late December sun,
Which today begins holding off the darkness
And moving toward fullness in the
Ever flowing dance of light and love;
Shine on us, that we who live in the shadows
May in the blue dawn experience these
Not as death and misery but
As layers of protection,
That our trust in you may deepen
In that quiet dark space.
For you hovered over the darkness and void
To make light and life.
Amen.

Week 1, Day 5

God of the soft first snow
The gentle white that
Covers everything, hushing the busy world,
And calling out your praise;
Grant us softness and a hushed awe
At the change of seasons
When we are compelled to pause for praise.
For you send the snow and the rain
To cover the earth,
Gifts for your creation,
Which we all receive.
Amen.

WATCHING (WITH HOPE)

Verb (used without object): to be alertly on the lookout, look attentively, or observe, as to see what comes, is done, or happens; to look or wait attentively and expectantly.

Verb (used with object): to keep under attentive view or observation, as in order to see or learn something; view attentively or with interest.

Noun: close, continuous observation for the purpose of seeing or discovering something; vigilant guard, as for protection or restraint.

Questions to Consider This Week

As you continue to ponder *what you are waiting for,* I invite you to read the following poem. How do waiting and watching go together? How are you waiting and watching in your life right now? How is this waiting a sign of your hope?

....

....

....

....

....

....

....

....

Week 2 Poem: Snowy Morning

gentle white falling, heav'ns soft gift
almost covering the land,
almost made new
and I'm adrift in thoughts of you.

every morning, rich foamy delight in a mug,
this morning scented cinnamon,
gifts of bounty and promise for toil
and I'm awash in your friendship.

woosh and wings and slack-jawed stare
catch it, catch it, I murmur behind the lens
hands shaking.

a brush of majesty,
unbidden,
and I'm transformed
already and again.

Week 2, Day 1

God, the newborn babe,
The Light of the World
Who let yourself be hid
In your mother's womb,
Darkness for nine months
That formed you;
Open the darkness for us
Let us not be afraid to be
Alone, held, formed.
Help us embrace this friend, darkness
For you yourself embraced
Darkness at the beginning
and the end of your life,
And you overcame it.
Amen.

Week 2, Day 2

God of the blinding sunrise
These fleeting moments when the sun,
In all its bright orange energy
Pokes its head above the tree line,
Above the neighbors shed,
To declare the night finally over;
Grant us eyes to witness your triumph
And hearts to bear your message,
To ourselves and to the world.
For you give us this daily bread of beauty and of hope.
Amen.

Week 2, Day 3

God of the deep red rose
A single long stem
With petals upon petals that
Unfurl in delicate surrender;
Grant us to see your beauty
Pausing to witness your creation's
Constant testimony
So that we may offer ourselves
in surrender to you.
For you inspire roses
And me to open up.
Amen.

Week 2, Day 4

God of the early morning birds,
Brown and grey feathered friends who stick around
All the cold and blowing winter,
And those color-patched marathon fliers
Here to nest as the world around them wakes up;
Grant us patience
to wait where we are
To endure a cold season or
To rest from the marathon of our work.
For in waiting and resting
We may be saved.
Amen.

Week 2, Day 5

God of the dormant lawn
Brown earth that appears dead
And is completely bare;
Remind us of the lushness of early summer
And of green lawns,
Refresh us with your love,
That we may be content in this season
Trusting in your work though it be hidden
From us at the moment.
For you bring forth life
When none can be seen.
Amen.

CELEBRATING

Verb: to observe (a day) or commemorate (an event) with ceremonies or festivities; to make known publicly; proclaim.

Questions to Consider This Week

As you continue waiting, what are you noticing? Are there ways that you can celebrate—either the season, or small moments that you recognize as gifts during this waiting time? Are you aware of God during these moments of celebration?

....

....

....

....

....

....

....

....

....

....

....

....

....

Week 3 Poem: Holidays

Swirly blue plates from the dollar store, one chipped
from daily service,
Sit prettily atop the silver bedecked table, leaf in
Expanded to hold the throb of guests;
Delicate gold-plated serving dishes, buried most
of the year,
Wink and shine in the flickering candlelight
Burning to delight the throng of friends.

Joyful greetings from the crowded doorway
Overhung with fresh pine boughs and
plastic mistletoe;
Soft pop of the green glass and the clinking of
Crystal goblets, filled carefully with festive bubbles;
Murmur of conversation amid forks to mouth and
Serving spoons scooping seconds of shared sides.

Baked apples and cinnamon rising
A warm dessert offering,
Melting whipped cream adds sweetness.
Fresh ground beans another,
More bitter, offering for balance,
While the cleanup crew rises to offer the service
of dish duty.

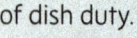

Week 3, Day 1

God of Peppermint Bark and Eggnog,
Those sweet treats of the season
Which delight us in decorative bowls
And fancy glasses;
Grant us hearts to see the small
Gifts of the season,
Your food and drink;
That we may receive joy
In our shared moments of sweetness.
For you give all good things.
Amen.

Week 3, Day 2

God of the holiday party and festive gatherings,
Those times when we gather for food and
Conversation in our finery,
When friends and family surround us in all
Their loud and weird glory;
Grant us hearts full of gratitude,
That we may not take your people,
Whom we love, for granted;
And that we may extend hospitality to those
Who are alone, grieving, in need,
Including ourselves.
For you are found in the gathering.
Amen.

Week 3, Day 3

God of the Christmas Tree,
That sturdy evergreen with presents piled underneath,
Grant us hearts of generosity
That we may share our burdens and joys
With those around us;
For goodness overflows
And we are filled when we give gifts.
Amen.

Week 3, Day 4

God when there is no Christmas Tree,
When the house is bare,
The space is empty,
the heart bereft of love;
Bear us up, O Lord.
For we need you when all around us
Are lights, toys, packages, and noise.
You promise you are even here, with us
And we are counting on you.
Amen.

Week 3, Day 5

God of those who weary of celebration,
We who want no more food, drink,
Gatherings of people chattering endlessly;
Grant us hearts of silence.
For then we can be thankful,
And generous,
And bear one another up.
Amen.

WAITING (IN DARKNESS)

Synonyms for *waiting*: alert, anticipative, anxious, apprehensive, breathless, eager, expecting, hoping, in suspense, looking for, on edge, on tenterhooks, prepared, raring, ready, vigilant, waiting on, watchful, with bated breath.

Questions to Consider This Week

As you continue pondering *what you are waiting for*, I invite you to consider how you are waiting. Do any of the synonyms for waiting listed above speak to your current experience? Has the thing you have been waiting for shifted? Has it arrived yet?

Week 4 Poem: In the afternoon

head pounding, neck aching, radio blaring
the ride home is a numb blur of
grays and browns, whizzing by
monotonous sounds sliding into one another
and as I take a breath, I'm parked in the drive and—

how did that happen?

slow, savor, see the gifts.
slow and notice breath:
my own miraculous inhale and exhale,
the breath of wind, unseasonably warm that begs the
windows be thrown open,
the joyous promise of spring,
the divine breath within that invites surrender and offers peace.

savor and enjoy sounds:
the crunch of little feet on packed snow,
the gentle trickle of melting and dirty piles responds to the sun,
child and canine voices carried on the wind, alive with play,
stillness that grows and presses comfortably.

see and receive gifts:
an afternoon lengthening before me,
delight on his face, digging rapturously in the white mounds,
concentration on hers as she enters the Lego world to create,
the hope of you, returning home soon.

to slow, to savor, to see is the gift.

Week 4, Day 1

God of the overcast morning
Where dawn wakes a weary pilgrim
Mumbling and grumbling before finally
Sliding back the covers and tossing out
Just enough light to see;
Grant us perseverance to walk
In that limited light,
Trusting in your full goodness and love
When obscured by thick clouds.
For you hide your full glory
From us now
But promise us face to face
And we trust you.
Amen.

Week 4, Day 2

God of the melting snow
The fading white piles
Disappearing slowly as warmth and light advance;
Grant us patience as parts of us seem
To disappear as life and circumstances advance.
For your warmth and light
Work to soften and dissolve the parts of us
That are not love.
Amen.

Week 4, Day 3

God of the people who fail you
We whose ancestors exchanged their own glory
For an image of a calf,
Who dimmed your light in others
Because they were different or
Because they could be used for something or
Because the fear in us is just so great;
Forgive us, Lord, for deeds done
And left undone,
For our part in it all and
Help us, Lord, to turn to you
As the only One who can make
Any of this right.
For your promises don't fail,
Even when we do.
Amen.

Week 4, Day 4

God of the ice-encrusted mornings,
When the sun rises enough to make
The whole blue tinted yard visible
And the glittering branches hang beautiful
And on the verge of breaking;
Grant us to experience
The love of your son,
Who has risen so that
Life may flow back into our icy hearts
And we may know our own beauty and
Brokenness more fully.
For you yourself hung on that edge
Of brokenness and chose to stay,
Being fully broken so we
Can be fully alive.
Amen.

Week 4, Day 5

God of the snow day,
That unexpected gift of a break in the routine
The chance to frolic outside,
Nap under a quilt, read by the fire, or
Drink hot cocoa during a board game;
Grant us the unexpected gift of your presence,
Which may inspire playfulness or restfulness
Within us.
For it is in these unexpected places
Where you offer us to yourself
That we can experience a taste
Of the good life.
Amen.

Bonus Sunshine Prayers

God of the Florida sun,
The paradise in February where
Strawberries are in season,
Visitors wear T-shirts, and
Natives clutch jackets close;
We give you thanks for this sunshine and
The chance to experience
Warmth out-of-season.
Give us refreshment and gratitude so that as we return home
Full of life and vitamin D
We carry your warmth and love
For your love travels as you never did,
to all the whole world.
Amen.

God of the Massachusetts sun,
That ordinary home in February
Where nothing edible grows in the ground (yet)
Where visitors come to ski and play while
Locals feed their fires and plant seeds inside;
We give you thanks for this sunshine,
Wan but steadily growing each day.
Give us patience and endurance
That as we wait for the turning of the seasons
We experience you with us.
For your creation tells the story of new life
And we watch it with eagerness.
Amen.

God of sunny days in late winter
When we get a glimpse of it all
Warmer temperatures,
Light a little later in the day,
Soft smells rising from moist earth;
Give us hope and endurance
For the tumult of spring,
When before the rising and blossoming
We witness the rains and whiplash
Of a season emerging.
For you do not tease us but
Remind us through gifts as small
As a sunny warm day
That your love endures forever.
Amen.

Spring

The Natural and the Liturgical Calendar

The Church calendar and the natural calendar flow together in beautiful harmony. The natural season of spring runs roughly March, April, and May (in the northern hemisphere). During this time frame two major seasons occur within the Church: Lent and Eastertide. Lent is the time of preparation before Easter—the forty days before it when we are mindful of our sins and need for God.

Spring begins with Ash Wednesday, where we are reminded that "from dust we came and to dust we will return." It ends as Holy Week begins; Palm Sunday, where we remember Jesus' triumphal entrance into Jerusalem on the back of a donkey; Holy Thursday, where we remember the Last Supper of Jesus with his disciples; Good Friday, the most somber of days, where we commemorate Jesus's crucifixion; and Holy Saturday, where we wait in suspense until at last Easter Sunday, and we can celebrate Jesus' victory over death itself!

This ushers in Eastertide, the fifty days after Easter, where we celebrate the arrival of the Kingdom of God through the death and resurrection of Jesus. I love this tiny detail, forty days of fasting and fifty days of feasting, because it reminds us that while we have work to do, there is much to celebrate and give thanks for.

A Season for Resurrection and Hope

Spring speaks to our hearts about resurrection and hope, particularly through our senses. We witness tender green shoots unfurl toward the strengthening light. Warmer days caress our skin as we bare arms and legs after a long season of jackets and jeans. From the purple crocuses braving through the snow, the bright red and cheery yellows of tulips and daffodils, the shy pinks and the blushing blues all the way to the pale lavender of the lilacs, heady on the bush, our eyes take in the beauty and wonder of God's creation made new. Birdsong, peepers, wind through the growing leaves, all whispering to us of the hope that life is fresh, and God resurrects what seems dead.

A Season of Tumult and Labor

In addition to hope and resurrection, spring speaks to us about the tumult of growing, the long and energetic days of work, and of God's extravagance in all the lush colors, sounds, and scents. We journey through cold but lengthening days, a growing mud season, and must endure more waiting before we eventually get to the blooming, the flowering of all things new.

There is so much to notice and to embrace during springtime. I encourage you to take in as much as you can about the outside world—what do you see, feel, hear, taste, and smell? I encourage you to connect with a church or a group of like-minded people who will help you to notice and see God in the seasons of Lent and Easter. Use any of the blank spaces in this section to record your own observations about the seasons, and let those observations shape your prayers.

Question to Consider in Spring: What Is Being Born in You?

As you are aware of particular sights and sounds this spring, I invite you to go deeper and ask what the gifts might want to say to you. Let the question for the season guide you, and provide a touchpoint for you to keep coming back to as you experience this season and reflect on all that unfolds.

On a lilac

Rolling off the tongue as a gentle exhale, the word itself
is a caress, filled with longing, anticipation of bloom
and scent. All winter, life is white; no green on the deck,
no leaves on the limbs, nothing from my outside inside,
in a vase. The view is clean and clear; the scent is cold,
warmed by dinner in the oven. The snows lie heavy with
a taunt: your sweetness must wait.

The sun smiles, basking over winter's insult until mankind,
ever despairing spring's arrival, awakens to the smell of new.
The snow trickles home with a whisper, not a bang. White
is banished and green emerges. Within the rush of the
promise lies another cruel barb: it's coming! But not yet.

The rain laughs at humanity, we so fickle to hope and
to have hopes dashed. The new turns muddy, the green
stays closed, and we are forced to hang on, balanced
between the valley of despair and the heights of hoping.

Then as we struggle, eyes closed and trust swimming
dangerously out of view—buds appear. Petals unfurl.
Life happens. No longer white, nor brown, but green,
green everywhere.

And with wild release, all creation sings: The promise is true! It's here now! And gloriously, the purple blossoms open and one by one by one, tumbling and falling together in a rush of lilac—the scent so heavy, perfuming my kitchen and my brain so that thought and pleasure mix and winter's taunt is obliterated. The sweetness of color, of scent that makes me drunk; this is the celebration of the promise that grows unbidden in the human heart.

Noun: an act or circumstance of entering upon an action or state; the point of time or space at which anything begins. *Adjective:* just formed; first; opening.

Questions to Consider This Week

As you ponder *what is being born in you*, I invite you to read the following poem. What things are beginning in your life? Where do you sense something new, even if you can't fully identify it yet? How do you respond to this new awareness?

....

....

....

....

....

....

....

....

....

....

....

....

....

....

....

....

Week 1 Poem: Beckoning

in the soft part of the night
as i am alone and dark
my heart hears yours and
soul to soul we whisper secret
longings and cry silent tears

across my cloudy soul, over the dew
dripped plains of my insides
the rays of sunlight fall
and i am shaken to depths beyond reach by
your ability to see without eyes

breaking through new earth hurts—
what can replace the pieces that
die on that journey? with a handful
of roses you urge me forward
i poke my way the pain lessened by your
beautiful gift

poised on new shores I shiver
from inside out
your sweet breath on my face
stills all and the
language of love needs no words
and I no longer fear

Week 1, Day 1

God of the crocus,
That eager one whose lovely face braves the snow
In response to the first tugs of light and warmth,
Bringing to the cold and wearied world a promise
 Of the more to come;
Grant that as we turn our faces to your son
In response to his first tugs of love and welcome
We may bring to a cold and wearied world
Your promise of more to come.
For in your love, we bloom.
Amen.

Week 1, Day 2

God of the grape hyacinths,
Those tender and tiny stems
Which support a multitude of
Glorious purple flowers;
Grant that we may tend carefully
Our own stems of faith,
So that we may in time
Witness our own glorious
And eventual flowering.
Amen.

Week 1, Day 3

God of the juvenile squirrels
Who leap and tumble
In exploration and exultation;
Grant us freedom in our own bodies and selves
To find you in the divine gift of play.
For there we may meet you
Like a little child.
Amen.

Week 1, Day 4

God of the hostas,
Whose broad tendrils
Unfold in due season,
Sharp pokes through mud before
The gentle work of shade and
Soft purple for bees can begin;
Cause in us sweet faith to leaf out,
That we may trust in your work within,
Both the pain of growth and the gift of rest.
For in you we find work and shade.
Amen.

Week 1, Day 5

God of the mourning doves,
Winged friends with a mournful coo
Who rise to the sky
In a whoosh of iridescent wings;
Give us the tune of lament
That we may bear witness
To sorrow and rise up
Toward you in our own iridescent glory.
Because you yourself wept
Before you rose.
Amen.

TOILING

Noun: hard and continuous work; exhausting labor or effort. Verb: to engage in hard and continuous work; labor arduously: to move or travel with difficulty, weariness, or pain.

Questions to Consider This Week

As you continue to ponder *what is being born in you*, I invite you to read the following poem. What are you working hard on in this season of life? What and how are you nurturing this thing that God may be calling forth from you? Is there a sense in which the work—your toiling—is an act with God?

....

....

....

....

....

....

....

....

....

....

....

Week 2 Poem: Ashes

Crumbles of what was
dark earth, dark matter, dark me.
Ashes.
Smaller, lighter, less; smeared heavy on the forehead
the press of another's hand very real. Flesh touches flesh.
Ashes.
Seeds of what might be
broken wings, broken light, broken me.
Pieces, parts, shreds; lifted by hands, held by love
the very mark of dirt, a promise.
Ashes.
Proof of what is
beautiful earth, beautiful light, beautiful me.
all, complete, whole. Touched by man and by God
something new.
Ashes.

Week 2, Day 1

God of the forsythia,
That bright yellow explosion
And unruly sign of spring;
Grant us so to see the wild bushes
Of our own ordinary lives,
And when faced with these unruly signs
May we respond as Moses did, by taking off our shoes.
Because this is holy ground, and you are here with us.
Amen.

Week 2, Day 2

God of the mockingbird,
Those who mimic all sorts
Of other sounds and songs
And whose enthusiasm keeps it
Singing through the night;
Help us to sing the songs of
Others when our own voices fail
And grant us to find our own
Songs to sing in the dark.
For you sing over each of us
And we are made fuller
In the sharing of songs.
Amen.

Week 2, Day 3

God of the dandelion,
That bright, ubiquitous announcement of spring.
May we notice what is everywhere and
Value that which intrudes upon the green of our
Perfectly cultivated lives.
For you sometimes show up like a weed
And invite us not to clean up first.
Amen.

Week 2, Day 4

God of the cappuccino,
The frothy milk swirled atop
The brown morning delight,
Grant us appreciation for all the gifts of the earth,
Plants and animals alike so that
We may enjoy goodness as it comes,
And in moderation.
For in slowing down and savoring
We may see things as they really are.
Amen.

Week 2, Day 5

God of the woodpecker,
Bright red tufts
Atop nail sharp beaks,
Those whose work is to hammer
In high and hard places;
Create in us a bright longing for justice
And zeal to throw ourselves into
The work you have given us to do.
Because we find ourselves
And you in places of our work.
Amen.

WAITING

Noun: a period of waiting; pause, interval, or delay.

Adjective: serving or being in attendance.

Questions to Consider This Week

As you continue to ponder *what is being born in you*, I invite you to read the following poem. What are you waiting for? How might the image of a pregnant woman change your perception of this waiting? How is God with you as you wait for this thing to be born?

....

....

....

....

....

....

....

....

....

....

....

....

....

....

....

....

Week 3 Poem: March is Mid

March is mid-season
>Despite calendar or weatherman;
Not the deepest cold
>Nor the full onslaught of color yet,
But brown, and moody
>A tumultuous whiplash of weather.

March is mid-sun
>An increase in light and longing;
Not the strength and length as the year's zenith
>Nor the watery and wan winter's rays,
But enough power to course through bare branches,
>And create patches for the dog's sprawl.

March is mid-melt
>The relentless creep of lion and lamb;
Not giant piles of white in the driveway
>Nor the soft broken earth of definite spring,
But alternately hard and frozen ground
>Perfect conditions for potholes and heartache.

March is mid-semester
      That ache of the incomplete;
Not the smell of new books, the feel of a new pen
      Nor the sudden burst of energy at the sight of the end,
But the slog through something important, and good
      And the temptation to give up.

March is mid-sentence
A thought and a feeling in process;
Not the satisfaction of the fully realized
      Nor the crest of a swelling wave
But the mind's activity, the heart's focus
      Again life's loves reordered.

March is mid-yawn
      The earth waking and us with it;
Not yet bright-eyed and bushy-tailed
      Nor dimly attuned to the life within
But a growing awareness gentle and slow,
      An occasional and vigorous shaking off of slumber
Blinking into the next season.

Week 3, Day 1

God of the hardy primrose,
That open smiling face
Supported by branches of broad leaves;
Grant us seasons of turning to you
With open countenances, that we may
Lean on the many who support us in this life.
Because our beauty and hardiness is
Intertwined with others.
Amen.

Week 3, Day 2

God of the tulip,
Those slender-necked cups of color
That grace walkways and tabletops;
Grant us flexibility,
That we may bloom in service where you have planted us,
For however long you ask us to.
For in service, we find ourselves
Cups of love to be poured out.
Amen.

Week 3, Day 3

God of the ruby petunia,
That deep red and double-blossomed glorious vine,
Grant us the double gifts of faith and hope
So that we may cling to you, the true vine,
Thereby remaining in the first of all gifts, which is love.
For as we are connected to you, we find freedom
To be our true and glorious selves.
Amen.

Week 3, Day 4

God of the weeping cherry,
Laden boughs dripping with pale colors
In the strengthening springtime;
Help us to see that our tears are beautiful,
And though in season we may be laden with them,
We can bow to you and be relieved.
For you gather all to yourself in beauty.
Amen.

Week 3, Day 5

God of the lengthening days,
Light and warmth stretching out
Minutes and hours before us,
Increasing everything;
Grant us more of you,
That as we bathe in your light and warmth
Everything increases.
For you are the source of growth
And you delight in the growth of your creation.
Amen.

RISING

Adjective: advancing, ascending, or mounting; growing or advancing to adult years.

Adverb Informal: somewhat more than: in approach of.

Noun: the act of a person or thing that rises.

Questions to Consider This Week

As you continue to ponder *what is being born in you*, I invite you to read the following poem. Are you aware of any transformations? Can you finally "see" with more clarity this thing that wants to be born? What signs of life are visible to you right now?

Week 4 Poem:
The Flowering of the Cross
(or what comes after)

Not one but two deaths, to hammer
home that we are but dust, as if
smearing ashes on the forehead just
wasn't enough.

A memorial service, followed by
another vigil, sandwiched between
math tests, Latin vocab and
baking bread.

Old stories heard fresh
reread and retold through
a book of wild creatures –
A Wild Hope indeed.

A retreat, beautiful and sweet
teenagers, also beautiful
but sometimes less than sweet and
flowers from him, just because.

Holy Week: a chance to walk through
the passion, not avert my gaze.
Witness suffering, together with my church
feel the sorrow, grieve the losses, wait.

Waking that morning. the only morning,
to feeble sunshine,
rushing wind, baskets of candy
pastel eggs, a new day.

Church again, and the same wooden cross
I touched then, was now
becoming something new
I had a part in creating.

We filed up, in groups and clumps
each of us bringing ourselves and a bit
of beauty. We touched and were touched in the
Flowering of the Cross.

Week 4, Day 1

God of the caterpillar,
The tiny green grub that eats and grows and eats
Every day, over and over
Until it spins its own cocoon,
Shrivels and dies,
Only to emerge a completely new and gorgeous creature
With wings that can carry it to worlds unavailable
To its former green grub self;
Grant us the patience, day after day as we eat and grow
and eat,
As we enter cocoons of our own making and wait,
With you, to die, and as we push forth into new worlds
On our new wings.
For you ate and grew, and died, and emerged glorious first.
Amen.

Week 4, Day 2

God of the monarch,
The king of those who journey 3,000 miles to Mexico
On paper thin wings and nips of beauty;
Grant us to know our own frailty,
To trust your Spirit who leads us,
To know our own strength, to beat our wings in freedom
of purpose,
And to sip the beauty you provide.
For in embracing our frailty and strength,
We embrace our true humanity.
Amen.

Week 4, Day 3

God of the peach tree,
Heavy with blooms
Already making the slow journey
From blossom into fruit;
Grant us perseverance and the roots
To sustain our own beautiful flowers,
That as we continue in you,
These may turn into good fruit.
For as we abide in you,
We bear your fruit.
Amen.

Week 4, Day 4

God of the lilacs,
The pale purple incense of spring,
Boughs that dip their heads in full blossom;
May we attract others being our full selves,
Rooted in your love, and as we open more and more
May we find our own heads dipping in praise.
For you are beautiful and you made us in your image.
Amen.

Week 4, Day 5

God of the neighbors on a walk,
Those we know and see around,
Who pop more into view as the weather warms;
Help us to be true neighbors
To love and serve those who you have placed in our lives
Whatever the season.
For you showed us how with your very life
And sent your spirit for this very purpose.
Amen.

Bonus Transition to Summer Poem: There Comes a Moment

There comes a moment.

Perhaps on a neighborhood walk, when you realize it's warm enough to take off your jacket.

Perhaps one evening under a luminous moon, with water a mirror for the heavens, you hear the peepers roaring to life.

Or one morning, sitting in a sunny patch of your worn-out sofa, looking across the front lawn and you see hues of green, where yesterday was mid-March frozen.

Maybe, it was last Tuesday with the flip of a page, a new month and what was

has lost its grip—just a bit, just enough—to let in a new you.

Once in a stained-glass church, with a chorus of voices, I soared like glorious freedom;
Once on a concrete bench, with a child sick, I sat grounded, like laborious love.

When this moment comes and whispers to you,
Open-handed, open-hearted, let it speak.

The world is greener now than yesterday.

Summer

A Note on "Ordinary Time"

The longest season of the Church year is the expanse between Pentecost[7] and Advent (the beginning of the Church year and the start of another cycle). This stretch of time, nearly half the year, is called Ordinary Time, and it's during this season we learn from Jesus' life and ministry, celebrate the life and power of the Holy Spirit, and practice living out our Christian calling.

The words ordinary and ordinal[8] come from the same Latin root *ordo-*, meaning order. The weeks of Ordinary Time are organized by ordinal numbers: the 1st week of Ordinary Time, 2nd Week of Ordinary Time, and so on. It's not that time between Pentecost and Advent is *not special* (and therefore "ordinary") but that the time is *ordered*. It's important and counted because this is when practice and growth happen.

Nearly all of summer occurs within Ordinary Time. It's worth considering how this season and all its beauty and gifts come to us in many seemingly ordinary ways.

A Season of Green and Growing

Summer is a time (at least in the north) when things are green and rich; there is evidence all-around of the growth that has taken place since the spring. Trees are fully leafed out, and shade is at its most abundant. Flowers bloom all season long, blossoms turn to fruit, and vegetables ripen in the sun. It's an easy season to appreciate the abundance of the earth!

---

7   Pentecost is the celebration of the arrival of the Holy Spirit in the early church, and the Spirit's presence and power in our daily lives. This occurs fifty days after Easter, usually late May or in June.

8   Ordinal numbers are 1st, 2nd, 3rd etc.

While these seemingly ordinary sights of nature—trees, flowers, fruits, vegetables—may be easy for us to take for granted as the weeks of Ordinary Time pass, there is an invitation to slow down, notice, and savor them. Spend half an hour in the shade of a grand tree, pick a bouquet of wildflowers, eat a peach with gusto, admire your neighbor's fresh tomatoes, all in an act of worship to the Creator and in appreciation of the growing process.

A Season of Play and Rest

Some of us have an adjusted schedule in summertime and can spend more time outside, eating al fresco, reading in a lounge chair, walking near the water, or just sitting for a few moments in the sunshine. It's a time when some of us go on vacation, spend time with family, enjoy recreational activities, but also slow down enough to take a nap or sleep in, and generally enjoy not being rushed.

But whether you have a flexible job or a differing schedule because of kids, have exactly the same schedule year-round, or have some level of chaos all year, summer is an invitation to both play and to rest. The longer daylight hours invite evening and outside activities of all kinds, and the intense work of spring has ended. Go ahead and enjoy some of the fruits of that labor!

Question: Where Do You See Signs of Growth?

As you are aware of sights and sounds this summer, I invite you to go deeper and ask what the gifts might say about your life with God. Let this question for the season guide you and provide a touchpoint for you to keep coming back to as you experience this season and reflect on all that unfolds.

Sitting with Grandma

S-A-I-N-T L-O-U-I-S Z-O-O. What does that spell, Grandma?
"St. Louis Zoo."

I sighed and sank onto the park bench, the peeling paint
tickling the backs of my thighs and the heat of the late
afternoon sun burning the back of my neck. My feet
dangled, swung back and forth; hers rested on the hot
concrete. My plastic jellies glittered purple; her toes
sparkled bright pink beneath rainbow straps on her
sandals. My hand-me-down cut-offs and strawberry
shortcake t-shirt evidenced the end of a long summer
day; her denim skirt and pale blouse stood impervious
to the heat and humidity. My small hand found hers
and our fingers interlaced. I twirled her thick wedding
band around her finger, wondering aloud when the
sea lion show would be over.

"Pretty soon, I would think," she murmured. I sighed
again. She angled her arm so that I could snuggle in
close. I tucked my legs underneath me and leaned to
trace the lines in the dark denim on her skirt. "How come
you didn't want to see the show, with everyone else?"

I shrugged. What could I say? With the afternoon heat ebbing away slowly, with me nestled snugly against her side, with no siblings or cousins to interrupt a moment's bliss, my heart sang happy. She slowly drew my thin bangs away from my eyes, letting her finger linger across my brow. "We'll, I'm glad. Do you want some ice cream?"

WEEK 1
BEAUTY

Noun: the quality present in a thing or person that gives intense pleasure or deep satisfaction to the mind, whether arising from sensory manifestations (as shape, color, sound, etc.), a meaningful design or pattern, or something else (as a personality in which high spiritual qualities are manifest); something excellent of its kind.

Questions to Consider This Week

As you *look for signs of growth*, I invite you to read the following poem. How is beauty a sign of growth? How might appreciating beauty be an act of worship? What is beautiful around you?

....

....

....

....

....

....

....

....

....

....

Week 1 Poem:
On a Strawberry

Soon, I think to myself. Very soon.

Sunshine dapples, shifting ever so slightly from watery to wan, from gentle to beaming, from soft to warm. Soon.

My daughter laughs with friends, giddy with excitement about the last day of school, murmuring plans for the summer. Soon.

My son digs fresh soil with me, relishing the turn of the earth's axis, slow and steady, poking holes for the beans. Soon.

My husband commences with his students, offering wisdom for the journey ahead, sharing memories from the year. Soon.

I inhale patience along with heady purple perfume, reveling in the glory of the last while eagerly anticipating the first. Soon.

The sun, as if she herself had finished a luxurious stretch and shaken her head like a dog out of water, realizes: It's time.

The morning, as a divine gift to humanity, hums. It's as if creation knows this moment, realizes this sacred reality: winter's bleak is banished, spring's promise is unfolded, all in the red jewel before me. In a field, in a squat, I give thanks: for the red, the essence of ripe. For the juicy, for the sweet. For the promise and the taste. For the miracle and the ordinary.

Week 1, Day 1

God of the peonies,
Velvety petals by the handful,
Heady, heavy, halcyon blooms;
Grant us the gift of wonder,
That by seeing grace and beauty all around
We may be your grace and beauty
To the mad, mad world.
Amen.

Week 1, Day 2

God of the Aspen,
Silver trunked beauty,
Whose hands wave and flutter
Specific hellos;
Grant us awareness of our
Own silvery beauty and
The gift of hospitality,
That we may uniquely greet
those we encounter.
For you yourself offer beauty and
Invitation to us all.
Amen.

Week 1, Day 3

God of the calla lilies,
Those regal and focused blooms,
Aware of their singular beauty and thus
willing to drop all pretenses of anything else;
Grant us an awareness of our own selves,
Such that we can proudly live into
The beautiful truth of who we are
Rooted in the knowledge of your love.
Because in this knowledge
There is freedom to let everything else go.
Amen.

Week 1, Day 4

God of the hummingbird,
That fleeting and iridescent flier,
Whose furiously beating wings require
The beauty and openness of a flower;
Grant us our daily beauty,
So that we may realize how our lives
Depend on your bounty.
For you delight in sharing your beauty and abundance.
Amen.

Week 1, Day 5

God of the ocean,
Which lies peachy glass at sunset,
When colors shift and fade by the second;
Help us to attend to the shifting patterns around us
Colors and love swirling endlessly.
For in you we find beauty
As well as ourselves.
Amen.

PLAY[9]

Noun: brisk, light, or changing movement or action; elusive change or movement, as of light or colors; freedom for action, or scope for activity; to move about lightly or quickly; to present the effect of such motion, as light or the changing colors of an iridescent substance.

Verb: to operate continuously or with repeated action; (informal) to comply or cooperate.

Questions to Consider This Week

As you *look for signs of growth*, I invite you to read the following poem. How is play a sign of growth? Do you find God playful? How might play connect you with God's heart?

_____

9   It's worth noting that Dictionary.com has over 60 definitions for the word play.

Week 2 Poem: Bike ride

C'mon, Mommy!
My limbs, awkward and unused, lacking a youthful litheness
I once took for granted, gently obey.
I balance tippy-toe, and the bike
wobbling underneath, patiently waits for me to settle.

My hands grip the handlebars and suddenly
it's my fifteen-year-old hands holding tight
and I'm off to visit Grandma Jeanne's.

How odd to be here and then.

Here, a bundle of six-year-old pent-up energy
zooms by, grinning as furiously as he is pedaling
and my face breaks into joy that is contagious.
Whee! I gather up speed and
the wind whips my hair and rushes my ears and
I am then thirteen and free,
sunshine and happiness awash.

Here, his young face lit with delight
as I push closer, and closer...
as I pass, the sheer glory of it all
is written in sparkling blue eyes.
Then I am ten, and unafraid,
wind and warmth, exploring
and feeling life as myself.

Here I am breathless,
laughter and a winter's long inactivity
catching me off guard,
and then I am breathless,
laughter and a lifetime of
possibilities before me.

Week 2, Day 1

God after the rain,
When all is fresh and refreshed,
Grant us times to pause after being filled
so that we may appreciate and soak in your love.
For you send rain to the earth for all things,
Including us.
Amen.

Week 2, Day 2

God of the Milkweed,

That slender orange and red-capped bush,

The only source of landing and launching for the
Monarch

Whose pods eventually burst open in giant milky puffs

To catch the breeze and travel;

Grant us stability of life and heart

So that those in our lives coming from near or far

Find a place to land and to launch,

And that our desires may burst forth and be carried by
your spirit

To places of fulfillment.

For you are both the place of safety and of adventure for us.

Amen.

Week 2, Day 3

God of the pool,
Crystal clear on a sunny day,
Cool water that refreshes as it supports
A floppy, purple inner tube;
Grant us days in the sun and in the water
That soak us in your love, and
Cleanse us from our own seriousness.
For you delight in our play.
Amen.

Week 2, Day 4

God of the snowbells,
Tiny white blossoms
That pour out and
Tumble down in long, draping vines;
Grant us freedom to grow and tumble and
Show forth your praise
With not only our lips
But our lives.
For you are a God of Life.
Amen.

Week 2, Day 5

God of the Gerber daisy
Bright faces turned
Toward the sun,
Opened in colorful abandon;
Grant us freedom to be fully opened
To you, our true colors exposed
And radiant as we turn and follow you.
For as we see you, we are seen and known.
Amen.

REST

Noun: the refreshing quiet or repose of sleep; a good night's rest; refreshing ease or inactivity after exertion or labor; relief or freedom, especially from anything that wearies, troubles, or disturbs; a period or interval of inactivity, repose, solitude, or tranquility.

Verb: to go away for a rest; to direct (as the eyes—to rest one's gaze upon someone); to let depend, as on some ground of reliance.

Questions to Consider This Week

As you *look for signs of growth*, I invite you to read the following poem. How is rest a sign of God's growth? How easy or hard is it for you to rest? How can rest be worship and connect you to God?

....

....

....

....

....

....

....

....

....

Week 3 Poem:
Penny, who is lying in the sun

Golden light, having thrown off night's chill
sprawls luxuriously over you.

As a majestic beast on the Serengeti, you
relax supine, poised to sniff the air and to receive
your subjects—slender blades of gold and green,
cheerful citizens content to bow and sway in your presence.

A crimson guest chitters at the feeder, his voice
tumbling and cartwheeling with the same
exuberance that roly-poly honey-colored offspring might;
it barely registers a flick of your silky and royal ear.

If this were another life, you might have a pride
of creatures to protect and feed and survey and groom.
But it's only this life, sunshine on a yard that waits patiently
to be mowed and trees that begin to shed summer's
work with a hint of future glory.

And I think maybe you have something to teach me
about being the king of this life.

Week 3, Day 1

God of the hydrangeas,
Whose riot of blooms
Blues, purples, pinks
Need two hands to cup them,
And who crave more water;
Help us to stay connected
To you, the river of life,
So that we too may thrive
And thus produce riots of virtue,
Peace, love, joy.
Because through you
We can discover our own true colors.
Amen.

Week 3, Day 2

God of anniversaries,
Those markers of events that mark us,
Grant us the gift of remembrance so that
We may not forget your goodness,
And we may be re-membered in the process.
For you yourself instituted a meal of remembrance,
Which you invite us into.
Amen.

Week 3, Day 3

God of anniversaries,
Those markers of events that mark us,
Grant us the gift of peace, so that as we
Acknowledge and remember painful moments
We may experience your goodness and be healed.
For you yourself experienced devastating loss.
Amen.

Week 3, Day 4

God of that sunset
(Aug 13, 2022, Salem, MA, harbor)
With the chatty but secretly worn-out passenger
Who confessed a hard life with a blended family of six,
And a Captain who smiled deeply through his beard,
And my husband and I celebrating 22 years of marriage,
All on a sailboat once owned by General George Patton,
Which now unfurled handsomely in the setting sun and
brisk wind;
Grant us to retain this spirit of thankfulness
When life is back to salads and lunchboxes and negoti-
ated bedtimes.
For you are a God of order and surprises.
Amen.

Week 3, Day 5

God of the retreat,
That time and place away from the busy-ness
And circumstances of our lives,
Grant us this gift of pulling back to be with you alone
So that we may re-enter our lives with clarity and
renewed vigor.
For you yourself withdrew on regular occasions
To seek your father.
Amen.

CONNECTION

Noun: association; relationship; a channel of communication; a group of persons who are connected, as by political or religious ties.

Verb (Connect): to join, link, or fasten together; unite or bind.

Questions to Consider This Week

As you *look for signs of growth*, I invite you to read the following poem. Why is connection necessary for growth? How are you connected in your life to yourself, to others, to God? How can you be more intentional about creating and sustaining connections?

....

....

....

....

....

....

....

....

....

....

....

....

Week 4 Poem: the way the ocean pulls

the way the ocean pulls
long and slow
scraping and kissing
the shore
like one deep inhale

the way the shells crunch
satisfying underfoot
as if hard steps can
ground out
shattered
and shared pain

the way the sky sings
expansive and open
wind whipping up
and calling
me out

Week 4, Day 1

God of the marigold
Puffs of orange and red
Whose sharp scent serves
To warn pests away from the tomatoes;
Grant us to allow the service of others,
To receive their protection and warning,
Even if it is sharp or we prefer
The pastels of spring.
For you created us all with beauty and work to do,
And we do well not to resist your creation.
Amen.

Week 4, Day 2

God of the lupine,
Flowering purple spires
Supported by a handful of leaves
On each stem
Splayed out like an open palm;
Help us so that with our knowledge
We would not tower over others but gently
Bow in confident love, and that our own hands and
Palms remain open and receptive to you.
For you did not tower over others
But offered your own self, your own hands
To be wounded for our healing.
Amen.

Week 4, Day 3

God of the cricket
That friend who hides in dark corners,
Yet fills whole rooms with her music that must be heard;
Have patience with us who hide and give us the grace
Of our own voices and songs, which eventually must be heard.
For you delight in the praise of your creatures.
Amen.

Week 4, Day 4

God of the milkweed
Shelter and sustenance for the king of the butterflies,
And which sends giant, delicate seeds attached to a
parachute of fluff
Into the backyard and the wider world;
Grant us stability that as we share with others
Homes and meals, both long and short term, the
Seeds of love would be carried far and wide.
For being rooted in love allows the flinging forth of
blessings.
Amen.

Week 4, Day 5

God of the milkweed tiger caterpillar,
Those black and orange hustlers, fluffy and ravenous ones
Who bustle to devour the milkweed leaves,
Grant us a lively community and sense of camaraderie
So that as we go about our daily lives under your protection
And with your provisions, we may thrive.
For even the least among us thrive in community.
Amen.

Bonus Benedictions

God of the still mornings
When light is diffuse through clouds,
Air hangs still and no leaves dance,
When crickets and birds greet the dawn
From the edges
And even the squirrels' usual
frenetic activity is muted;
Grant us stability of heart
To sit with what is
And to press in when we might
Prefer to move along.
For you are at work in the stillness
And invite us in.

God of the late summer day,
When skies are clear, the sun warms your creation
without overheating
And the trees still dance greenly;
Grant us rest and play in these days so that we may be
nourished by your love
And receive your abundance.
For you delight in giving gifts.
Amen.

Autumn

Liturgical Note

As we transition from summer to autumn, we are still in the longest stretch of the Church calendar, Ordinary Time. It's not until the very end of autumn that we move into Advent, the Church's New Year.

A Season to Gather and Release

Autumn carries some of the "order" of summer—days and weeks still marked as the "sixteenth Sunday/week in Ordinary Time" or whatever—but with autumn comes the harvest. Things we have seen growing in summer are now complete: flowers have bloomed and now turn to seed; vegetables have formed and are now ripe. We gather the literal harvest that the Earth has produced and which we had a part in cultivating, celebrating abundance and bounty, gifts and hard work. We also gather the metaphorical harvest of friendship and family as we gather for celebrations.

Autumn is also a season of release. Once we gather the harvest, we begin to put the garden to bed. The trees shed their leaves—parts of themselves that have grown and served them well and served us too with shade and fruit. But these leaves are no longer needed during the cooler months; in fact, if the tree does not release the leaves, it will die in winter![10] We witness this process in the world around us and also embrace it within ourselves. During autumn, we are invited to examine our lives and release any habits or ideas or even people who no longer serve us in this next season of life.

---

10   This process has something to do with the amount of chlorophyll produced, and a process called *abscission*, which has the same Latin root for the word scissors.

A Season of Equilibrium and Change

Autumn also carries some of the "ordinariness" of summer, with days of warmth even as the nights get longer and cooler. The season begins at the equinox, that day in September when the days and nights are equal, approximately twelve hours of each. We walk through the shortening days of the season until the shift to winter and the darkest season. We are invited to think about the ways in which our lives have an important equilibrium, and what we might do to support that.

But autumn is also a season of great change: the temperatures change, the light changes, the landscape changes with first the leaves changing brilliant colors and then falling dramatically to reveal bare branches. We change our clothes from shorts to sweaters to hats and gloves. We are invited to consider the way our lives are changing and embrace that change.

Question(s)s to Consider in Autumn: How Do You See Equilibrium and/or Change in Your Life? Where are You Invited to Support Equilibrium or Embrace Change?

As you are aware of the natural world this autumn, I invite you to go deeper and ask what you are aware of within yourself? Let this question for the season guide you and provide a touchpoint for you to keep coming back to as you experience this season and reflect on all that unfolds.

INTRODUCTORY POEM

Crystal Moments (On being 13)

The light has faded, along with its promise, and you, snuggled up under ocean covers— light deepening to purple, hiding the mysteries beneath—hopeful for a bedtime chat.

Slats of morning march inevitably across the floor, and with arm flung across your face, you murmur: not quite yet.

A mother's litany grows as the morning: brush teeth? pack lunch? gym clothes? Questions of love and worry: Are you ready? With ponytail and careless shrug, you step into the day.

The direct beams are a direct contrast to your non-answers. A whole day apart, a whole world within. Sunshine warms, cold seltzer bubbles and together we sit.

Shuffling the broccoli, a window into your high-low-rainbow-
buffalo:[11] a good teacher, group work, funny classmates.
Twilight falls upon your chocolate eyes, clear and deep.

Back to bedtime, and the hope for a back scratch.
Brother and dog nearby, kisses, hugs, and belly button
checks all given, and the night softens around you.

---

11   This is often what we ask each other at family dinners: high is best part of
the day; low is something "bad" (we try to elaborate - disappointing? Made you
angry? sad?); rainbow is something beautiful or when you saw God; buffalo is
something random. This often involves bodily functions....

EQUILIBRIUM

Noun: a state of rest or balance due to the equal action of opposing forces; equal balance between any powers, influences, etc.; equality of effect.

Questions to Consider This Week

As you consider *where you see equilibrium in your life*, I invite you to read the following poem. How are equilibrium and steadiness connected? How might you live into this steadiness, going into a season of change? Where is God in the midst of this?

Week 1 Poem:
Caim (circle of protection)

I stand and point
   down, toward the floor
and I breathe.

Beginning here, a birth of
   air and light
and I move.

The circle widens
   as I follow the sun
clockwise and in harmony.

I stumble and pause
   afraid—to keep moving
or to stay still. How will I know?

Unbroken, I move again
   and the line is drawn
clarity for what lies within and without.

Life in motion and
   the lines blur:
the safe must be released, the foreign embraced.

"Look for the helpers."
　　An unbidden guest offers consolation
with a soft gaze:

he, long-forgotten
　　and no longer hoped for
bears my Sisyphean stone.

The circle, incomplete, though enough—
　　wobbles as I,
but my protector does not.

Back to where all good journeys start,
　　a fully formed cycle is
complete and I breathe.

Week 1, Day 1

God of the late summer morning
When fall is in the air
But only a hint, and
There is a deposit on the promise of a warm sun,
When everything is paused
After the big inhale of summer,
Ready to begin the long exhale into fall;
Grant us patience,
To wait with the seasons as they move slowly
And to wait with you as we move slowly toward maturity.
For the Kingdom of God is a slow-moving and
Sometimes delicate experience.
Amen.

Week 1, Day 2

God of the mountains,
Whose brown ridges contrast
With the bright sky,
Harsh outlines caused from
And cause of a harsh landscape;
Grant us to accept the contrast of our lives,
Places where harsh lines
Meet blue expanses,
and grant us peace in the midst of a harsh life
And harsh circumstances.
For you are big enough to hold it all.
Amen.

Week 1, Day 3

God of the dead bugs,
Those who appear suddenly
On our floors or in the corner,
All legs upside down in
A cartoonish version of death,
And those we kill with a swatter
Or heavy book or our own shoe;
Forgive us the violence we
Willingly or not—do to others who are
Different than we are,
Or who inconvenience us.
For all your creatures have
A purpose, and deserve some peace
In life, if not death.
Amen.

Week 1, Day 4

God of the squirrels
Those pests of the yard who intrude and
Take up space as playful, seed burying annoyances,
Grant us wisdom to see the pests in our lives as from you,
And who may serve a purpose we can sometimes never know,
And grant us the grace to accept all parts of ourselves,
even our annoying ones.
For you work in mysterious ways and act out of love for
our sake.
Amen.

Week 1, Day 5

God of the late summer day
When we realize how much light we are losing,
And the air carries a chill, the shadows tugging us
Toward the inevitable change and into winter;
Grant us rest and peace on these days
So that we may more fully surrender our lives to you and
Trust in your seasonal work.
For you are always inviting us into the next moment.
Amen.

CHANGE

Verb: to make the form, nature, content, future course, etc., of (something) different from what it is or from what it would be if left alone; to transform or convert; to become different;[12] the passing from one place, state, form, or phase to another.

Questions to Consider This Week

As you *consider where you see change coming in your life*, I invite you to read the following poem. How are change and steadiness connected? How might you embrace this change, for a season? Where is God in the midst of this?

....

....

....

....

....

....

....

....

....

....

....

---

12 Note that change can be active, as in the first definition, or passive; you can change, or you can be changed.

Week 2 Poem:
the way the leaves light and dance

the way leaves dance
swaying and sighing melancholy
thin, spidery and fragile

the way light dances
streaming and bursting through
holes, cracks, and tears

the way that I love
wobbling and triumphant some
translucent with effort

the way that you love
rising and setting ever
over, around and through

Week 2, Day 1

God of the draught
That season when rain is absent
And all creation begins to groan
For your living waters;
Grant us to desire only you
And to turn to you in seasons of dryness.
For you send rains to water the earth
And you sent your Spirit to refresh our souls.
Amen.

Week 2, Day 2

God of the still mornings
When light is diffuse through clouds,
Air hangs still and no leaves dance,
When crickets and birds greet the dawn
From the edges
And even the squirrels' usual
Frenetic activity is muted;
Grant us stability of heart
To sit with what is
And to press in when we might
Prefer to move along.
For you are at work in the stillness
And invite us in.
Amen.

Week 2, Day 3

God of the geese
Those migrating ones
Honking and flapping toward
A more hospitable landscape,
Driven by changes in the light and air;
Grant us to witness their flight,
Blessing them along the way,
And grant us hearts attuned to
Your gentle tugs and changes
Perhaps imperceptible to the eye but
Known in the eye of our hearts.
For you are the God who calls
And who guides all your creatures.
Amen.

Week 2, Day 4

God of the mid-day
The pause between the freshness of the morning
And the work of the afternoon,
When we slow down to eat,
To talk, to refocus;
Grant us wisdom as we reflect
And let go of things from earlier
And recommit to things still to come.
For you invite us into pausing
Before the next thing.
Amen.

Week 2, Day 5

God of the hazelnut, the small package
Of perfect nutrition for many creatures and
Earthy spice for morning drink;
Grant us who are small to be who we are
And through our integrity provide what others need,
And flavor our relationships with goodness.
Because what you created is useful and delightful.
Amen.

GATHER

Verb: to bring together into one group, collection, or place; to bring together or assemble from various places, sources, or people; collect gradually; to pick up piece by piece; to wrap or draw around or close; *(Nautical)* to gain way from a dead stop or extremely slow speed.

Questions to Consider This Week

As you consider *what you are invited to gather in*, I invite you to read the following poem. Can you articulate what it is you are gathering? How do you feel about this thing? Is God at work as well, gathering with you?

....

....

....

....

....

....

....

....

....

....

....

Week 3 Poem: On a Pomegranate

You wouldn't know the complex trail of seeds within,
a whole universe hidden, snug and safe within a waxy
   sheen of red.
You couldn't tell the days of waiting, the hours of silence,
   the minutes
of longing as each seed burst into life, and then began
the painstaking process of becoming a full seed.
You can't imagine the slow fingers of nature,
unfurling beauty one drop at a time.

I notice the curve, trace the mystery, and touch the fullness;
each globe a weight that I gently pass to young hands.
I ponder the culmination of sunlight and water, the gift of the soil,
labor of man and earth—all contained within my palm.
I receive the work of nature, the bountiful and generous offering,
absurdly delighted with such splendor.

Preserving the moment, savoring the tangy pop
grinning with young faces... the fruit becomes a feast
a celebration, soon only a sweet memory.

Week 3, Day 1

God of freshly baked bread,
The great equalizer and comforter,
Whose aroma pleases as it
Delivers nourishment;
Grant us grateful hearts
As we eat together
And celebrate your great sacrifice
Your body, the bread of heaven,
Broken for us.
For as we eat, we remember
And are fed.
Amen.

Week 3, Day 2

God of those we love who have died
Meet us as we laugh, remember, grieve
For those who are gone from our sight.
Grant us to trust in your mercy,
Rest in your love, and
Hope in your eternal life.
For we are wounded by love,
As you were.
Amen.

Week 3, Day 3

God of the blue jay
The nosy, beautiful and bossy birds
Who live in the borders
And land imperiously at the feeders;
Grant us freedom to use our outside voices
Calling forth goodness and righteousness
From our friends and neighbors.
For our bossy impulses can be tamed
In the working of good for others.
Amen.

Week 3, Day 4

God of the apple,
The plentiful and crisp smelling fruit of the season,
Which falls to the ground in abundance
And from that extravagance
Comes apple cider;
Give us wisdom to not only see but to appreciate
And delight in your abundance, O Lord, which is all
around us.
For you lavish gifts upon your creation
And nothing is wasted in you.
Amen.

Week 3, Day 5

God of the pokeweed
That gorgeous and sturdy stem
Loaded with dozens of deep purple berries
Which delights the eye but poisons the stomach;
Give us your eyes of compassion
That we may see what is beautiful and
What is toxic in our own lives,
And give us wisdom to embrace the beautiful
And resist the toxic.
For you desire us to thrive.
Amen.

RELEASE

Verb: to free from confinement, bondage, obligation, pain, etc.; let go: to free from anything that restrains, fastens, etc.; to allow to be known, issued, done, or exhibited.

Questions to Consider This Week

As you consider *what you are invited to release from your life*, I invite you to read the following poem. What are you being asked to release? Who is asking you to release something? Are you willing to say yes to this release?

....

....

....

....

....

....

....

....

....

....

....

....

....

....

....

Week 4 Poem: Bedtime on a Sunday

The house itself sighs into the quiet.
Appliances cease their
whirring, tumbling, cleansing,
their constant working finally at rest.

Carpets worn from the traffic of
little feet running, kneeling, playing
a family in motion, now lie proudly
displaying criss-crossing vacuum lines.

Bunk bed holds curiosity and kindness,
two little bodies snuggled together,
while bins of toys neatly line
underneath, hidden in order.

King bed invites,
with crisp white sheets and sham
pillows arranged just so,
whispering, "Come."

I sigh into the quiet.
Strivings cease their
pulsing, tumbling, tossing,
my frantic mind finally at rest.

Spirit worn from the traffic
of much worry, caressing, and holding
tightly, begins to release and now
looks lovingly to the gifts around.

Heart holds curiosity and kindness,
two gifts given so that the
dullness and pain hidden underneath
may be transformed in order.

The King Himself invites,
With a warm word and
me arrayed just so,
whispering, "Come."

Week 4, Day 1

God of the long shadows
Those friends whose fingers point us
Toward forgiveness as the time winds down;
Help us to embrace the coming darkness,
The shorter days and times of quiet rest.
For you ask us to let go and move into
A season when your deep and hidden work
Can continue within and you yourself showed us
This hidden way.
Amen.

Week 4, Day 2

God of the drizzle
Days of rain that fall like love
Coming and going with cloud cover
And soft grey light;
Help us to embrace gratitude for your gifts
And life-giving provisions,
Even when it seems dreary or interminable.
For you are with us in all conditions
And offer us necessary respite with the
Shift from sunshine to rain.
Amen.

Week 4, Day 3

God of the falling leaves,
Those colorful jewels released
From the trees for its own protection;
Grant us such freedom to embrace
The falling in our own lives,
The beautiful yet unnecessary for next season
Parts that must drift down to become
Nourishment again.
For you sustain us in growth and in diminishing.
Amen.

Week 4, Day 4

God of family and friends,
Those whom we love,
Those present with us, those separated by miles,
And those no longer with us.
As we gather to feast with gratitude,
Give us the gift of yourself,
That by being together we may experience
Joy and by eating together we may be filled.
For you yourself celebrated with family and friends
And know the gift of the feast.
Amen.

Week 4, Day 5

O God, who bears the title Christ the King,
You who alone bears the weight of love
For all your creation;
Grant us, your true subjects,
The freedom to come and serve you
As we love and serve those you created.
For your kingdom is coming
And we wait upon you.
Amen.

Endings and Beginnings

It is fairly obvious that each season is different from one another—this is part of the journey, learning to see and appreciate those shifts in light, temperature, and all of it. But as we finish out one year and begin again, circling the same landscape, *we discover that each year is different too*. We are not the same as we were one year ago, and this winter is not identical to the previous one. This is a part of the journey as well. In fact, it is a way to mark our growth as we notice what is similar to and different from this time last year.

As you finish one year and prepare to move into the next, it can be helpful to remember the seasons are cyclical, not linear (despite our modern calendar). You aren't limited to the December into January moment as a new start—you can have a beginning and an ending at any point. If you started in spring, that becomes your place to pause and remember last year as you begin to move into this one. Or if you put this book down in summer and are picking it up in winter (two years later!) then this is your invitation to look back as you look around and ahead.

It can also be helpful to look back at anything you may have recorded for yourself, either in this book or in a journal, or in some other way you tend to keep track of the days. Reviewing an old planner or the calendar on your phone or your photos from the last year can provide surprising and ultimately helpful insights into how you spent your time and what was important or significant about the past year.

Here are some questions to guide you in the space of moving year to year:

As you look back to the season you started in, what do you notice now about this same season?

Winter: do you notice any similarities in weather (first snow day? How or do you celebrate the winter solstice, the shortest day of the year?) Are there similarities in your travel or holiday plans and experiences? Are there emotions this year that are different than last, as the cold days wear on? What were you waiting for last year, and how is that similar or different from what you are waiting for this year?

Spring: are there similar plants coming to life? Are there differences within the same perennials? Do you notice the same smells and sounds, or are you noticing something different this year? Is there something that was being born in you last spring that is now growing? What is being born this year in you?

Summer: are there different things growing in your yard or garden? How is the environment—the weather, the neighborhood, your own house—the same or different as last year? Where are you hoping to see signs of growth this year in yourself?

Autumn: do you have any particular experiences you hope to enjoy again—leaf peeping, pumpkin gathering/carving, apple picking? What were you doing in your life this time last year, and how is it different from what you are doing now —did you move to a different house or state? Start dating anyone or break up with someone you loved? Are there things you released last fall that you can see benefit from? Is there leftover pain from something that was lost to you?

As you move from year to year, one of the most helpful things I can offer is the invitation to be gentle with yourself. There is no need for—and no benefit to—judging our own experiences. We simply want to notice what we notice, give thanks for the gifts, and if there is something that needs attention or tending, we turn gently toward it. I hope that this whole book helps you to pay attention to the seasons, the world around you, and opens up space for you to see the life that is within you. Whatever season you find yourself in now is an opportunity to step closer and see what's there and what unfolds. That is my prayer for you.

One final thought: Goodness Grows

Goodness and beauty take time to grow—while evil can come in quickly and destroy. This is part of what inspired me initially and motivates me nearly every day to keep watching. Beautiful things take time to grow and unfold. We can witness this in nature if we watch, and as anyone who works with their hands in the dirt knows, it takes time for something good and beautiful to grow, and we have a part in nurturing it. This includes ourselves.

It takes patience to watch the world around you begin to thaw, grow, bloom, fruit, and flower, turn to seed, finish with a fall. It takes patience to observe ourselves in a similar manner and begin to learn how to nurture our own life and growth. This is one of the benefits of spending intentional time with the seasons: it can be a surprising portal into our own inner landscape.

You may be resistant or afraid to let yourself see what lies within. You may worry about the depth of emotion or the lack of any emotion inside; perhaps there is trauma, deep wounds that feel raw and wild, threatening to undo you if you even peek in. If you are brave enough and honest enough, you might be surprised and overwhelmed at the goodness and beauty you find there too.

Acknowledgments

The process of writing a book, of producing some new and creative thing into the world only happens with support. I had have so much of that in my life and in the book writing process!

Thank you to my mom and dad, my siblings, cousins, aunts and uncles, grandparents, and all who gave of themselves to form me into a person capable of paying attention to the world. I love you all! Special thanks to my mom Christy, for her unconditional support, not only of this project, but of my life.

Thank you to the family I married into, for raising such a great guy, and for supporting me along the way!

To my long-time, real-life friends on Marco Polo, Jen and Sarah, and to my sister Kate, with whom I share the daily ups and downs of life: thank you three for being there, for loving me and supporting me through the process of birthing a book.

Thank you to Mark and Nina, who listen deeply to me when I need a friend. To my spiritual director Sue, and mentor Susie, both of whom make space for me to notice God in my life, I am profoundly grateful.

Thank you to my church community, Trinity Northshore Anglican. I love worshiping with you on Sunday mornings; your faith is such an encouragement to me, and it's a complete joy to walk the weeks with you all. Thank you to the Edelweiss group, whose prayers lift and sustain me.

Thank you to Mother Wendy and Mother Jen for your love and care; thank you to Father Tim for your sermons which God uses each week to deepen my faith and awe, and for the beautiful forward to this book.

Thank you to Yvonne Mimmo for coming into my life and seeing what I could not. By helping me transform my physical space, you gave me not only a beautiful office and home, but you were part of the work that allowed my creativity to bloom. Thank you too to Eddie for all the hard work and support!

Thank you to the reNEW writing community, particularly Rachel Britton, Tammy Gerhard, and Deb Dufek. This community is a treasure of generous kind-hearted people who support one another— my writing and my life have been enhanced by your support.

Thank you to Wendy Murray for that writing workshop in February 2020, which brought clarity and focus to my writing. To the subsequent writing group which helped sustain that focus, Sue, Lindsay, Melissa, Carol—you ladies inspire me! I appreciate all our dinners, where we listen to each other and share our deepest lives. Jane, you are a lovely addition to this group.

Thank you to Beth Coombes (and to Sue, for the introduction) for the stunning watercolor images used in this book and on the cover. You are a true artist, and it was a delight working with you (and I loved our business meeting at the pool!)

Thank you to Pete Whitten for the gorgeous cover design. Thank you to Ian Drummond for the photos of the watercolors and for the headshots. Thank you to Melanie Chitwood for the thoughtful and professional editing.

Finally—last but not least—thank you to Alex and David, who show me what's possible in the world, whose questions and conversations I treasure, and whose lives I'm proud to watch unfold. And to Ian, my love. How can I possibly express my gratitude for all of your selflessness, support, and care over these last twenty-four years? You make me a better person, you fill my life with joy, and I anticipate marveling at the world with you.

Resources to Help You Further Embrace the Seasons

Spiritual Rhythm by Mark Buchanan

The Next Right Thing Journal by Emily P. Freeman

Seasons of Waiting by Barb Hill

Sacred Ordinary Days by Jen Giles Kemper

Wintering: The Power of Rest and Retreat in Difficult Times by Katherine May

Enchantment: Awakening Wonder in an Anxious Age by Katherine May

Daily Prayer: Praying with the Corymeela Community by Padrig O'Tuma

Return to the Root by Joyce Rupp

Divine Hours by Phyllis Tickle

Liturgy of the Ordinary by Tish Harrison Warren

Seasons of a Family's Life by Wendy Wright

About the Author

Jennifer spent much of her life observing the world around her. As a child of the Midwest, she was grounded in routines of an extended family and rhythms of the Catholic Church, and as an adult she continues learning new seasons in the Northeast. Beauty and nature have always called to her, and this book is an answer to that call.

To find out more about Jennifer or to drop her a note visit **www.jadrummond.com**

About the Artist

Beth spent her whole career as an emergency room nurse. At the age of 60, she challenged herself to take up watercolor painting, just to see if she had an ounce of talent. She has since gone on to produce thousands of beautiful images on greeting cards that are accompanied by her words of encouragement which brighten the darkest of days. She has lived in Salem MA for nearly her whole life with her loving husband. She is always surrounded by her beautiful family including her daughters, son, grandchildren, inlaws and siblings.

Connect with her at **elizabes@comcast.net**